W9-BEU-785

FUN FACT FILE: US HISTORY!

20 FUN FACTS ABOUT THE GOLD RUSH

By Joan Stoltman

Gareth Stevens
PUBLISHING

Please visit our website, www.garethstevens.com. For a free color catalog of all our high-quality books, call toll free 1-800-542-2595 or fax 1-877-542-2596.

Library of Congress Cataloging-in-Publication Data

Names: Stoltman, Joan, author.
Title: 20 fun facts about the gold rush / Joan Stoltman.
Description: New York : Gareth Stevens Publishing, 2019. | Series: Fun fact file: US history! | Includes index.
Identifiers: LCCN 2018001279| ISBN 9781538219096 (library bound) | ISBN 9781538219072 (pbk.) | ISBN 9781538219089 (6 pack)
Subjects: LCSH: California–Gold discoveries–Juvenile literature. | California–History–1846-1850–Juvenile literature.
Classification: LCC F865 .S855 2019 | DDC 978.4/04–dc23
LC record available at https://lccn.loc.gov/2018001279

Published in 2019 by
Gareth Stevens Publishing
111 East 14th Street, Suite 349
New York, NY 10003

Copyright © 2019 Gareth Stevens Publishing

Designer: Sarah Liddell
Editor: Mariel Bard

Photo credits: Cover, p. 1 Everett Historical/Shutterstock.com; p. 5 Wikipeder/ Wikimedia Commons; pp. 6, 17 ullstein bild Dtl./Contributor/ullstein bild/Getty Images; p. 7 (newspaper) Soerfm/Wikimedia Commons; p. 7 (photo) Bobak/Wikimedia Commons; p. 8 Droll/Wikimedia Commons; p. 9 Fæ/Wikimedia Commons; p. 10 Stock Montage/ Contributor/Archive Photos/Getty Images; p. 11 Durova/Wikimedia Commons; p. 12 JohnRandale72/Wikimedia Commons; p. 13 Jim Feliciano/Shutterstock.com; p. 14 coronado/Shutterstock.com; p. 15 optimarc/Shutterstock.com; p. 16 Hulton Archive/ Stringer/Hulton Archive/Getty Images; p. 18 Fanfo/Shutterstock.com; p. 19 Hulton Archive/ Stringer/Archive Photos/Getty Images; p. 20 Optigan13/Wikimedia Commons; p. 21 Irina Meliukh/Shutterstock.com; p. 22 Connormah/Wikimedia Commons; p. 23 Howcheng/ Wikimedia Commons; p. 24 Elizabethmaher/Shutterstock.com; p. 25 SuperStock/SuperStock/ Getty Images; pp. 26–27 Fine Art/Contributor/Corbis Historical/Getty Images; p. 29 Godot13/Wikimedia Commons.

All rights reserved. No part of this book may be reproduced in any form without permission in writing from the publisher, except by a reviewer.

Printed in the United States of America

CPSIA compliance information: Batch #CS18GS: For further information contact Gareth Stevens, New York, New York at 1-800-542-2595.

Contents

Words in the glossary appear in **bold** type the first time they are used in the text.

The Start of the Rush

On January 24, 1848, a carpenter named James Marshall discovered gold on John Sutter's property in California. Sutter and Marshall tried to keep the discovery quiet, but it didn't stay secret for long. Just a few months later, stories of gold on Sutter's land were showing up in newspapers.

Many people, including Sutter's employees, began mining the area in search of this rare precious metal. **Squatters** looking to find gold soon took over Sutter's land, destroying his crops and killing his livestock.

The man who was there for the start of the gold rush was later ruined by it. By 1852, Sutter was **bankrupt** and his property was destroyed.

5

FACT 1

A cook boiled Marshall's gold nugget to prove it was real!

James Marshall found the gold at Sutter's Mill, a sawmill he was constructing on John Sutter's property. Cook Jennie Wimmer boiled one of the pieces in **lye**, and because the nugget wasn't ruined by the lye, they knew it was real gold!

There was gold in California's riverbeds because thousands of years of weather had loosened it from the ground and washed it down the Sierra Nevada.

This local newspaper, called the *Californian*, announced the discovery of gold on March 15, 1848.

CALIFORNIAN
BY B. R. BUCKELEW.

SAN FRANCISCO, MARCH 15, 1848.

GOLD MINE FOUND.—In the newly made raceway of the Saw Mill recently erected by Captain Sutter, on the American Fork, gold has been found in considerable quantities. One person brought thirty dollars worth to New Helvetia, gathered there in a short time. California, no doubt, is rich in mineral wealth; great chances here for scientific capitalists. Gold has been found in almost every part of the country.

Marshall Gold Discovery State Historic Park, California

FACT 2

When newspapers announced the discovery of gold, few people believed it!

Fake stories about gold had been printed before, so people didn't think this discovery was real! The truth spread quickly around California, but it took longer to reach the East Coast.

FACT 3

President James K. Polk sparked a huge migration to California in 1849.

To prove his discovery, James Marshall sent his gold to the president. In December 1848, Polk announced to Congress that the gold was real. His words were printed around the world, and people rushed to California.

President James K. Polk

A member of the US military brought Marshall's gold from Monterey, California, to Washington, DC, for the president to see!

About 80,000 people came to California in 1849. These prospectors were called forty-niners.

Many early prospectors didn't know what they were doing!

People looking for minerals, such as gold, were called prospectors. Miners from Chile and Mexico who came to California often taught Americans how to prospect.

By the 1860s, more than 300,000 people had moved west to California.

FACT 5

Thousands of people walked for about 6 months to get to California!

Prospectors often started in Missouri or Iowa after traveling on the Ohio River or the Mississippi River. Heading west, they walked alongside oxen pulling wagons filled with supplies.

Structures couldn't be built fast enough, so some people worked and lived in tents!

FACT 6

San Francisco's population grew from around 1,000 in 1848 to over 20,000 just 2 years later!

Ships from all over the world unloaded passengers in San Francisco. Between the new arrivals and the people looking to make money off them, the city became a major port in the west!

FACT 7

Abandoned ships lay buried under the streets of San Francisco!

Most prospectors were not heading home any time soon, so the ships they'd used to get to California sat empty in the harbor. The ships were later sunk, and parts of the city were built over them!

About 62,000 people came to California by boat in 1 year alone. Some were Americans from the East Coast, but most were from other countries, such as China and Australia.

FACT 8

The simplest tool for finding gold was a big metal pan!

Early prospectors used a method called panning. They scooped up mud, rocks, and hopefully gold into the pans. Then they carefully washed away the mud, which is lighter than gold, leaving behind the precious metal—if they were lucky!

Claude Chana discovered gold in Auburn, California, in 1848. Today, this statue of Chana panning for gold stands in Auburn.

13

Boomtowns popped up almost overnight all over California.

People built towns wherever they struck gold. But once the gold ran out and more was found somewhere else, the miners moved on and built a new boomtown. All that remained was a deserted "ghost town."

Bodie, California, began with around 20 miners and grew to about 10,000 people by 1880. But just 2 years later, its population dropped to about 3,000.

As the months passed, prospectors had to dig deeper and search through about 200 buckets of dirt a day!

Miners tried strange tricks because they so badly wanted to find gold.

"Gold grease" and other gold-finding tools promised to make users rich—but they were **shams**. The grease claimed that gold would stick to prospectors' bodies as they rolled down hills, and they'd be rich when they reached the bottom!

All About Miners

FACT 11

Most of the people who moved west during the gold rush were men!

In 1852, more than 90 percent of prospectors in California were men! They quit their jobs back home, thinking they could get rich quickly and easily. But most ended up working from sunrise to sunset and didn't make very much money.

Miners left their families behind in search of gold, but many didn't know how difficut the job would be.

Miners were known to place bets on anything, including bear fights, card games, and horse racing. They lost a lot of money—and gold—that way!

Many miners spent their gold as fast as they found it!

Miners worked up to 16 hours a day, 6 days a week, and it was back-breaking labor. Some just slept, ate, and worked. But many turned right around and spent the gold they'd just worked so hard for!

Miners ate so many oysters that fisherman had to find more somewhere else!

Because they thought oysters were fancy and a sign of wealth, miners spent their money and ate a lot of them. Fisherman had to travel farther up the West Coast to find more to feed the hungry miners!

Legend has it that one miner who had just made it big in Hangtown, California, ordered the most expensive items on the menu—eggs and oysters—cooked up into a dish called the "Hangtown fry."

In 1850, immigrants made up about one-quarter of California's population!

Immigrants paid millions of dollars to California.

In 1850, California forced immigrant miners to pay a $20 tax (about $600 in today's money) every month. This tax was eventually **repealed** and replaced by a much lower tax on Chinese miners only.

FACT 15

California's first millionaire wasn't a miner!

Samuel Brannan owned a general store on John Sutter's land when gold was discovered there. Knowing he could profit off it, he spread the word about the discovery and then made his fortune selling everything miners needed, including pick axes and shovels.

Brannan's store

Brannan's general store earned him a lot of money. He sold up to $5,000 (about $150,000 in today's money) in goods and gear to the miners each day!

Selling food could make more money than mining for gold!

Most miners couldn't cook because women usually did that. As a result, groceries and cooked meals could be sold for crazy prices! Lucy Stoddard Wakefield made $240 a week selling pies. That's more than $7,000 in today's money!

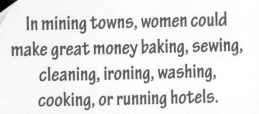

In mining towns, women could make great money baking, sewing, cleaning, ironing, washing, cooking, or running hotels.

FACT 17

The inventor of blue jeans made it big during the gold rush—but not by selling jeans!

Levi Strauss (of Levi's jeans fame) owned a store in San Francisco where he sold goods such as blankets and clothing. His family in New York sent him products other stores in California didn't have, which helped his business.

Strauss had been living in San Francisco since 1853. It wasn't until 1873 that he and Jacob Davis invented blue jeans.

FACT 18

The easy gold on the surface was mostly gone by 1850!

After the gold people could find by panning or **sifting** through the dirt was taken, prospectors had to work harder to find their treasure. This meant coming up with new ways to get gold, such as hydraulic mining.

Hydraulic mining used powerful hoses to blast water at hillsides to loosen dirt and, hopefully, gold.

On average, about $60 million worth of gold was found each year during the 1850s!

But this gold wasn't found by lucky people. Now it was found by companies that could afford expensive machines that drilled into the earth, blasted hillsides, and crushed stones that contained gold.

Much of the gold in the Sierra Nevada was deep underground. Gold mining became an **industry** with machines, tools, mills, and big money for big companies.

FACT 20

The gold rush brought people to California from across America and from more than 25 countries.

It was one of the largest movements in human history. And with so many different **cultures** all in one place, California was, and still is, very **diverse**.

Everyone who came to California, whether by sea or on land, wanted the same things: wealth and a better life.

Traveling from Far and Wide

ARGENTINA

AUSTRALIA

CHILE

CHINA

ENGLAND

FRANCE

GERMANY

GREECE

The gold rush brought people from around the world to California. Here are just some of the countries from which they came.

IRELAND

ITALY

MEXICO

NEW ZEALAND

PERU

PORTUGAL

RUSSIA

SANDWICH ISLANDS (HAWAII)

SCOTLAND

SPAIN

TURKEY

San Francisco, 1850

California Changed Forever

When the gold rush started, the United States had just gained California from Mexico, but it wasn't a state yet. It didn't take long, though! The population boom from the forty-niners helped speed up the process, and on September 9, 1850, California was added to the United States as the 31st state.

California was the most powerful state in the west thanks to the gold that had been found there. This money held a lot of power over the government. California continues to be a diverse and powerful state today.

EUREKA

CALIFORNIA

The California **coat of arms** shows a miner at work near the Sacramento River below the Sierra Nevada.

29

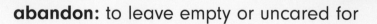

abandon: to leave empty or uncared for

bankrupt: unable to pay money owed

coat of arms: a special group of pictures that belong to a person, family, or group of people that are shown on a shield and have a certain meaning

culture: the beliefs and ways of life of a group of people

diverse: differing from each other

industry: a group of businesses that provide a particular product or service

lye: a strong chemical used to make soap

migration: movement from one place or region to another to live or work

repeal: to do away with

sham: something that is not what it appears to be and that is meant to trick people

sift: to go through something very carefully in order to find something useful or valuable

squatter: someone who settles on land without consent from the landowner

For More Information

Books

Hall, Brianna. *Strike It Rich! The Story of the California Gold Rush.* North Mankato, MN: Capstone Press, 2015.

Landau, Elaine. *The Gold Rush in California: Would You Catch Gold Fever?* Berkeley Heights, NJ: Enslow Elementary, 2015.

Shoup, Kate. *Life as a Prospector in the California Gold Rush.* New York, NY: Cavendish Square Publishing, 2017.

Websites

The California Gold Rush
www.pbs.org/wgbh/americanexperience/features/goldrush-california/
Learn more about this exciting event in US history.

Gold Rush Overview
www.parks.ca.gov/?page_id=1081
Read more about the gold rush on California's Department of Parks and Recreation website.

Publisher's note to educators and parents: Our editors have carefully reviewed these websites to ensure that they are suitable for students. Many websites change frequently, however, and we cannot guarantee that a site's future contents will continue to meet our high standards of quality and educational value. Be advised that students should be closely supervised whenever they access the internet.

Index